YOUR
OWN
MYSTERIES

praying your life through the rosary

Philip Armstrong, C.S.C.

ave maria press  Notre Dame, Indiana

© 2004 by Ave Maria Press, Inc.™

www.avemariapress.com

International Standard Book Number: 0-87793-838-5

Cover and text design by Brian C. Conley

Printed and bound in the United States of America.

Library of Congress Cataloging-in-Publication Data
Armstrong, Philip, C.S.C.
    Your own mysteries : praying your life through the rosary / Philip Armstrong.
        p. cm.
    ISBN 0-87793-838-5 (pbk.)
1. Rosary. 2. Mysteries of the Rosary. I. Title.

    BX2163.A76 2003
    242'.72--dc22

                                        2003021520

The Rosary is meant to be a prayer that leads us to Christ and into union with God. If it only locks us into a meaningless circle of mechanically recited prayers, the Rosary is not achieving its purpose. And Mary would be the first one to tell us to find a better way to God and love of neighbor. . . .

We should feel comfortable allowing ourselves a certain flexibility with the Rosary, as the U.S. bishops noted in their 1973 pastoral letter, *Behold Your Mother: Woman of Faith*. "Besides the precise Rosary pattern long known to Catholics," they write, "we can freely experiment. New sets of mysteries are possible."

Thomas Thompson, S.M.,
and Jack Wintz, O.F.M.
Catholic Update, July 2002

Contents

Acknowledgments

The publication of any book requires far more than the author's painstaking preparation of a manuscript. Many persons are involved in the overall process, from its inception until the book is in the hands of the reader.

I am grateful for the encouraging response of those who heard bits and pieces of the manuscript in various presentations, especially when listeners applied the mysteries to their everyday lives, like Pat McBride, who put the Wondrous Mysteries to the test while jogging.

Two longtime close friends in Holy Cross, Brothers Joel Giallanza and Renatus Foldenauer, read several versions of the manuscript and kept me on course by their supportive but honest and effective critique of the text.

Father John Phalen, C.S.C., president of Holy Cross Family Ministries, formerly the Rosary Crusade and Family Prayer apostolate begun by the great Rosary proponent Father Patrick Peyton, C.S.C., provided not only enthusiastic encouragement for the project but agreed to contribute a foreword to the book.

My religious family showed its unflagging support, especially through Br. Robert Fillmore, provincial of the Midwest Province of the Brothers of Holy Cross.

Ave Maria Press publisher Frank Cunningham welcomed the manuscript and editorial director Bob Hamma guided its early journey through the process. He then turned it over to the experienced and creative eye and imagination of editor Dan Driscoll, to whom I owe special thanks for his always efficient expertise and energetic good humor.

To all the family and friends whose affirming words and attitudes have given me the motivation and strength to continue, a monumental thank-you.

And I must not fail to acknowledge that more than once I felt the certain presence and encouragement of the Mother of us all, showing me how to persevere with trust as she did, seeking to make her Son better known and loved. If I have been a useful channel toward that end, it is enough.

Foreword

Brother Philip Armstrong, C.S.C., is a man of prayer and reflection who offers in this book some simple suggestions on how we might vary the Mysteries of the Rosary and expand them to include more of scripture and more from our own human experience. Giving talks and reflections on Mary and the Rosary, he became aware of how his use of the beads had evolved. He was, for example, praying over the lives of Holy Cross religious buried in the community cemetery. He was allowing portions of the Psalms and Isaiah to guide his Rosary reflections. His missionary experience of the African culture in Ghana was providing him inspiration. Even long before Pope John Paul II wrote his Apostolic Letter, "The Rosary of the Blessed Virgin Mary" (October 2002), offering us the Mysteries of Light, Brother Philip was seriously engaged in the question of alternative mysteries.

The letter of the Holy Father implies what has always been true: the laity decides the ultimate makeup of the Rosary. The faithful of the church will ultimately either accept this suggestion to broaden their view of the Rosary and make it part of their prayer, or reject it, leaving the traditional mysteries in place. It seems when the Pope makes a nonbinding and humble suggestion, people listen attentively. And because the Mysteries of Light do supply something of what has been missing of the public life of Christ as we contemplate the mysteries, it is very likely that the official Rosary has been altered for good. Time and the practice of those who use the beads will tell.

Of course, the Pope's addition to the traditional mysteries of the Rosary suggests to us all that composing alternative mysteries is acceptable. What this book asserts is that the scriptures and our own life experience offer a wealth of possibilities for fashioning mysteries which are personally significant and spiritually enriching. We can "contemplate the face of Christ," as the Holy Father says, in scripture and in the daily events of our own lives.

Something he expresses has relevance here: ". . . our heart can embrace in the decades of the Rosary all the events that make up the lives of individuals, families, nations, the church, and all mankind; our personal concerns and those of our neighbor, especially those who are closest to us, who are dearest to us. Thus the simple prayer of the Rosary marks the rhythm of human life."

Brother Philip Armstrong has been an author, teacher, administrator, missionary, provincial superior, assistant superior general, formator and spiritual director, retreat director, and speaker. He has been a Holy Cross religious for more than fifty years. His use of the Rosary over those years has acquired a very practical characteristic that he skillfully explains here.

It is most appropriate that a religious of Holy Cross should offer these alternative mysteries of the Rosary, as one of the best known promoters of the Rosary was also a member of the Congregation of Holy Cross, Servant of God Father Patrick Peyton. Father Peyton's motivation came from his seminary experience of being healed of life-threatening tuberculosis through the Rosary and the intercession of Mary. He lived his entire fifty-one-year priesthood thereafter promoting the Family Rosary around the world through the creative use of huge rallies and radio, television, and the film media.

In fact, there is a strong tradition of Marian devotion in the Congregation from the time of our founder, Venerable Basil Moreau, and that of the priest involved in the founding of the University of Notre Dame, Father Edward Sorin. As a recent biography of Father Sorin indicates, his custom was to write a letter concerning some important decision at the university, then place it on the Mary altar and pray (most likely the Rosary) over it. Father Peyton, who inherited a Rosary from Father Sorin, took up the same practice for his worldwide Family Rosary ministry. After praying the Rosary over his proposed letter, Father Peyton would trust the inspiration he received from Our Lady when he decided whether to send the letter as it was or to alter it or to cancel the project. He always considered Mary his guide. His themes were "The family that prays together stays together," and "A world at prayer is a world at peace." September 15, the feast of Our Lady of Sorrows, is the Congregational feast day.

May the reading of this short book inspire us to use the Rosary in the creative ways revealed by Brother Philip. The Rosary has given consolation to millions in its traditional form. Now with the addition of the Mysteries of Light concerning the public life of Jesus, it is even more provocative as a prayer of contemplation. May our own experimentation with alternative mysteries of the Rosary enliven our life of prayer and our devotion to Mary, the Mother of God and the Mother of the church. And may our commitment to Jesus Christ her Son, vital and active in our life, find new expression as we rediscover the Rosary.

Rev. John Phalen, C.S.C.
President, Holy Cross Family Ministries
North Easton, Massachusetts

1

Why Alternative Mysteries?

On October 16, 2002, in a move that took nearly everyone by surprise, Pope John Paul II promulgated an encyclical, *Rosarium Virginis Mariae*, the entire subject of which was the ancient prayer form known as the Rosary. Just as exciting was his introduction of a new set of mysteries to join the traditional *Joyful*, *Sorrowful*, and *Glorious Mysteries* and to be known as the *Luminous Mysteries*, or "Mysteries of Light." The encyclical, unlike most teaching letters that are addressed from the pope to bishops around the world, was aimed at "bishops, clergy, and the faithful," opening its rich content and pastoral counsel immediately to all the faithful (see *Rosarium Virginis Mariae* [*RVM*], inside address).

The Rosary has been promoted and prayed in the Roman Catholic Church since its approval by Pope Pius V in 1569. Separating fact from legend regarding the origin of the Rosary is not a simple matter. Were the beads handed to St. Dominic by the Blessed Mother?

Pragmatic and very human explanations carry as much weight as the unexplainable. "Medieval piety in the West developed the prayer of the Rosary as a popular substitute for the Liturgy of the Hours" (*Catechism of the Catholic Church* [CCC], 2678). A large percentage of the population at the time could not read, so the church suggested that while saying the *Paters* and *Aves* people reflect or meditate on events in the life of Jesus and of his mother Mary. This was meant to attract people to meditative prayer. It is said that a Carthusian monk divided the 150 Ave Marias of the full fifteen-decade Rosary into separate groups of ten, each with its own *mystery*. The 150 Hail Marys represented the 150 hymn-prayers of the Psalter, all of which were incorporated into the weekly chanting or recitation of the Liturgy of the Hours in contemplative monasteries and convents. Individuals who were unable to read could thus reflect on themes—mysteries—from the life of Jesus and Mary in lieu of praying the entire Psalter.

The mysteries attached to the Rosary were called *Glorious, Sorrowful,* and *Joyful* because of the events recalled in those particular sets. The Glorious Mysteries celebrated Jesus' resurrection and ascension, the coming of the Holy Spirit, and the assumption and coronation of Mary. The Sorrowful Mysteries noted Jesus' agony in the garden, the scourging and crowning with thorns, the carrying of the cross, and the crucifixion. The Joyful Mysteries proposed events surrounding the announcement by Gabriel to Mary that she would be God's mother, her visit to her cousin Elizabeth, the birth of Jesus, and his presentation and later finding in the Temple. Church authorities saw the Rosary as "an epitome of the whole gospel," expressing devotion to the Virgin Mary (see *CCC*, 971). To everyone's surprise, Pope John Paul officially introduced for the first time another set of mysteries, the Luminous Mysteries, or Mysteries of Light, focusing on the public life of Jesus: Jesus is baptized in the Jordan; Jesus manifests himself at Cana; Jesus proclaims the Kingdom and calls for repentance; Jesus is transfigured; and Jesus institutes the eucharist (*RVM*, sec. 21).

Mary is integral to the Rosary in that she was associated with her son throughout the events of the gospel and was his partner in the sacred history that led to our salvation. The Rosary, then, is not exclusively her prayer, but one in which she is featured alongside Jesus, helping achieve his mission on earth. The Pope explains in his recent encyclical, "The presence of Mary remains in the background," but "the role she assumed at Cana in some way accompanies Christ throughout his ministry" (*RVM*, sec. 21).

Is there more than one way to pray the Rosary? Several ways, as a matter of fact. Most people are familiar with the original and most popular form, namely, reflecting on sets of mysteries proposed by the church to go along with and enrich the repeated recitation of the Our Father, Hail Mary, and Glory Be. This becomes the content of prayer recited with others or prayed silently while fingering the five decades of the Rosary. "Meditation engages thought, imagination, emotion and desire. . . . Christian prayer tries above all to meditate on the mysteries of Christ, as in *lectio divina* or the Rosary" (*CCC*, 2708).

What has been good enough for nearly 450 years surely still ought to be good enough. Why, then, suggest a major change in the approach to the principal way in which the Rosary is used as prayer?

For hundreds of years the three traditional sets of mysteries have fueled countless recitations of the Rosary. Numerous books, even very recent ones, have been written elaborating on each of these fifteen scenes from the gospel. Since the Pope's promulgation of the Luminous Mysteries, additional books have been written augmenting the settings and implications of each. Whether the Rosary's origin is wholly human, wholly divine, or a combination of both, it has over the years been one of the most popular devotions in the church.

After the Second Vatican Council (1962–1965), by reason of a new emphasis placed by the council fathers on the liturgy and on renewal and adaptation in the priesthood and religious life, the focus of common prayer in the church was aimed toward the liturgy, whether the Mass itself or the Liturgy of the Hours. Popular devotions such as benediction, novenas, vigils, litanies, special prayers to particular saints, and the Rosary lost much of their immediacy and gradually most died out as regular practices, both in church and privately. Yet far from conflicting or competing with the liturgy, the Rosary "sustains it" (*RVM*, sec. 4). Because of its scriptural ties, the Rosary complements liturgical prayer.

It seems, however, that, as with many elements of Catholic life given new emphasis by the Vatican II renewal, the faithful saw continuing value in the use of the Rosary, and many sought to enhance its recitation even more appropriately by the application of the mysteries to modern Christian life.

Yet, there seemed to be no movement toward updating the Rosary. The Rosary was the Rosary; the mysteries were the mysteries. The suggestion of the U.S. bishops in 1973 that it is permissible to fashion new mysteries is a challenge apparently not taken up with serious effort even today (see the quotation from Thompson/Wintz, p. 3), though as Pope John Paul notes, "every individual event in the life of Christ . . . is resplendent with the mystery that surpasses all understanding" (*RVM*, sec. 24). Rather, the Rosary rapidly lost popularity within the anti-establishment culture of the seventies, just about the time Karol Cardinal

Wojtyla was elected pope. He declares in *Rosarium Virginis Mariae* that, ". . . on October 29, 1978, scarcely two weeks after my election to the See of Peter, I frankly admitted: 'The Rosary is my favorite prayer. A marvelous prayer! Marvelous in its simplicity and depth'" (*RVM*, sec. 2). With the dawning of his twenty-fifth anniversary as pope, John Paul wished to honor and encourage the use of his favorite prayer by proclaiming October 2002 to October 2003 as "The Year of the Rosary" (*RVM*, sec. 2).

It was only when, a few years ago, I began to reflect anew on the traditional sets of mysteries that I became conscious of an anomaly: though the mysteries referred to events in Jesus' and Mary's life that dealt with the infancy and early childhood of Jesus, his passion and death, and his resurrection and the time following (including Mary's death and assumption into heaven), not a single mystery invited reflection on happenings in the later years of Jesus' "hidden life," or the public life of Jesus up to his passion. To me, this didn't make sense. I asked myself whether I could put together alternative mysteries that would fill these gaps. Eventually, after much consideration, I did come up with such mysteries, plus many other sets commemorating various elements of life that touch on the presence and influence of God, Jesus, and Mary in our daily experiences.

So, it is in response to a personal need that I propose the free use of alternative mysteries. Yet, I recognize my problem has also been that of countless others, as I have spoken both publicly and privately on the concept of alternative mysteries and have found enthusiastic support for pursuing the idea. To facilitate that, both for myself and others, I have gathered my reflections into the chapters of this book. That Pope John Paul II and I have surfaced similar ideas almost simultaneously is no doubt more than mere coincidence. The results may providentially contribute to the enrichment of prayer through the Rosary for untold numbers of individuals.

I have dealt with new mysteries on which to reflect while praying the Rosary. But there are other ways to pray the Rosary than by associating particular events with each decade recited. The person praying may envision Mary's role in each mystery, whether or not it seems to involve her directly. The individual may concentrate on the meaning of the words of the familiar prayers recited. He or she may let the words of the prayers slip by almost unconsciously in a total contemplative silence in the form of the prayer of awareness of presence, of friendship, of "holding hands" with Jesus and Mary. Or the person praying may concentrate on world peace, someone's health and welfare, one's own personal needs, whatever factors influence one's life at the time. The form of the Rosary is not meant to take precedence over prayer, but to assist it, so whatever way a person uses the Rosary to facilitate prayer, that use is valid and worthy.

In proposing several new sets of mysteries and suggesting that beyond them are unlimited mysteries (made possible by using creative imagination aided by inspiration), I do not wish to minimize the three traditional sets that we as Catholics and as pray-ers of the Rosary have grown up with, nor do I mean to ignore the new Luminous Mysteries. The traditional ones, for many, have simply "worn out," and the same threadbare images appear and reappear in the mind of the one praying, while the beads slip more and more mechanically through begrudging fingers. Distractions have become more common than creative representations of this or that mystery. The final decade is, regrettably, often concluded with the realization that little attention has in fact been given to what was being said and done for the past ten to fifteen minutes. Often, the Rosary is abandoned altogether as beyond the ability of the individual to pray properly. The Pope tries to address this problem by introducing the Luminous Mysteries "to help the faithful to understand [the Rosary] in the richness of its symbolism and in harmony with the demands of daily life" (*RVM*, sec. 28). He means for the Rosary to be rooted in and rise out of our lived experience day by day.

Though offering a new approach to an old devotion, I am well aware that prayer is an intimately personal activity, and that one's spirituality depends entirely on how the relationship between God and the individual evolves and develops over the years. Your priority while engaged in any form of prayer is always the growth of your personal relationship with God as both you and God, through love, make it happen. The Rosary, like other prayers, is a means to an end. In whatever way the means can be directed toward achieving the end more perfectly for you, you have to feel free to move as you are led by inspiration. Do not consider any of the following sets of mysteries inflexibly and irreversibly set in stone any more than you would the traditional and now the Luminous Mysteries. As you grow more comfortable and familiar with further alternative approaches to praying the beautiful devotional prayer known as the Rosary, move into your own applications of suggested mysteries with their explanations and interpretations; let the Holy Spirit and Mary guide you along the paths in which they, through the Rosary, lead you. As the pope urges, "let the mysteries on which you reflect, whatever they are, help you to pray in harmony with the demands of your daily life" (*RVM*, sec. 28). The pope encourages people of all walks of life to "take up the Rosary once again . . . in the light of Scripture, in harmony with the liturgy, in the context of your daily lives" (*RVM*, sec. 43). The Rosary is nothing if not relevant to you at every moment in the unfolding of your life.

Throughout the book I quote from the *New Revised Standard Version* (*NRSV*) of the Old and New Testaments. Those accustomed to using the Bible to facilitate prayer will have their own favorite versions and should by all means use them. It is interesting and enlightening, though, to compare various translations on occasion.

A minor but practical suggestion: in order to carry about with you the possibility of praying new sets of mysteries, create for yourself a mnemonic device to help you remember the five mysteries in each set. As in memorizing the lines and spaces of the treble clef in music, very trite but effective sayings or associations serve as helpful ways to remember which mystery follows another. Of course, there is always the option of writing them out in abbreviated form and sticking them into the Rosary case, available every time the case is opened for prayer.

The commentary accompanying the mysteries in this book is not intended to be read aloud. Rather it can serve as background material for reflection during group recitation of the Rosary. Ideas from these paragraphs, if not the entire content, or the leader's own commentary may, for example, prove useful in introducing an alternative mystery for the first time within a group recitation setting. This book is meant to help you learn how to delve into your own spirituality and plumb the depths of its potential in further developing a more effective and engaging prayer life.

Thus, my purpose in this book is, as was Pope John Paul's in his encyclical, to carry forward in concrete and practical form the suggestion that new mysteries be created for popular adoption. It is my hope and prayer that you will find useful ideas elaborated in the following chapters. What has worked for me in an unanticipated way can, I believe, also help you. The same Blessed Mother is the mother of us all because she is the mother of Jesus who lives within us all. Her life was immediately, intimately, and intricately bound up with the mysteries that impacted the life of her son. She knows of our devotion to her and her prayer and, like the Holy Spirit, she will see to it that our human weaknesses will be compensated as she carries our requests, gratitude, sorrow for sin, and praise to God, who was the source of every blessing in her life and is as well for each of us.

2

The Wondrous Mysteries

What a rich field we have from which to harvest events from the public life of Jesus! Think of the possibilities for finding topics to ponder while praying the Rosary.

Here I propose five "wondrous" *situations* or *themes*. There exists such an abundance of incidents in Jesus' life among the people, why should we not broaden the scriptural references we have available to us for our meditation? The Pope has done so with his Luminous Mysteries.

I call the situations I have chosen the *Wondrous Mysteries*:

Jesus Encounters the Desert
Jesus Forms a Community
Jesus Heals and Restores Life
Jesus Teaches with Authority
Jesus Feeds the Multitudes

These topics draw our attention to Jesus as he begins his public ministry, but only after he has spent time in prayer and solitude and has come to terms with his vocation. Then, confident of the direction he must take, he begins to gather followers who will support and assist him in his mission. Out of his fresh understanding of who and what he is—the very presence of God in this world—he begins compassionately to restore wholeness and life to those whom he encounters, including three who have died. He speaks out of certitude and self-assurance, not out of the hollow power of a title or office, and not reliant on legalisms. He provides food for those who follow him, nourishment for their bodies and their souls. Each of these mysteries is a source of wonder to all of us as we reflect on the gospel accounts. Even more personally, doesn't each of these situations tie in somehow with similar challenges and responses at certain times in your own life?

Let's examine each of these Wondrous Mysteries more closely.

1. Jesus Encounters the Desert

Can you picture Jesus coming up out of the Jordan, newly baptized, having made contact with his cousin John and hearing God's approval? Can you see him, drawn by the Spirit into a personal retreat to deal with all those marvelous things going on in his imagination and his heart? He treks out into an inhospitable wilderness. This event encompasses more than just the literal period of forty days Jesus might have spent in the wilderness. Forty days here could mean Jesus spent a "lengthy time" apart in prayer and reflection. Thinking this way, it is easier to come to terms with Jesus' fasting during the extent of his retreat. Use, as you wish, the references to the temptations by Satan and the visitation by angels, but even taken figuratively they are rich sources for reflection.

I believe Jesus goes "on retreat" to experience a process into which he is led by the Father and by which he comes to confront an increasing sense of his unique identity as God, yet—of the essence for us—as truly and fully human. Also, he must discern his proper response as a human to the persons and goods of this world. We find this search typified in his baptism and the recorded temptations. Who is Jesus, we are asked, vis-à-vis the world and those whom he encounters in it? Both of these realities, confronted realistically and through prayer, help lead him to a clear recognition and formulation of his mission on earth.

How does Jesus respond to his maturing sense of confidence and its accompanying implications, including responsibilities? We can ask ourselves about our own call and discernment. How long did our discernment take before enough clarity was apparent to lead us to move confidently in a particular direction? How does Jesus come so assuredly to a sense of who he is and what he is to be and do in this world? As he does so, he is very much aware of the treatment traditionally accorded prophetic voices in Israel.

2. Jesus Forms a Community

Following his retreat in the wilderness, Jesus returns to daily life, not as a carpenter in Nazareth where he grew up, but as a wandering preacher based in Capernaum. His objective is to announce that God's kingdom is tangibly present. He invites the people to exercise a spirit of repentance so as to share in the new form of the ancient covenant God made with the people of Israel. Jesus assumes the role of prophet.

His first item of business is to identify and recruit helpers who are sympathetic to his mission, who will live simply, travel about with him, and be personally supportive of him. We observe that Jesus chose a most unlikely cast of characters, a fact that throughout the gospel confuses the authorities, whether representatives of traditional Judaism or of the Roman occupational forces. Even his own relatives wonder about him sometimes.

What is it that enables Jesus to call on strangers to abandon their livelihoods to follow him? By following this charismatic but equally enigmatic young leader who senses a special call from God, can they somehow find fulfillment and a bright future? How do they know?

3. Jesus Restores Health and Life

Everywhere Jesus goes he encounters the suffering of humanity. It draws from him a response so strong that, beginning with his mother's appeal to him at Cana, he cannot stop doing what he knows he can do to alleviate people's ills, whether the cause is sin, disease, or external evil. The gospels reveal Jesus' numerous healings, and even three occasions on which he restores life. In each case, evident faith and dire need arouse compassion in Jesus. He shows he is not in the business of miracles for their own sake. He does not heal to draw attention or to advertise his evangelical message, but to witness God's loving presence and its demanding implications.

What convinces Jesus he has the right and the ability to cure on his own authority, and to do so whenever he finds conditions deserving of the exercise of such a gift?

4. Jesus Teaches With Authority

Several times the evangelists note that Jesus "taught with authority, not as the scribes" or other Jewish leaders. In the eyes of the people, those men taught with power, that is, they interpreted life and the multiple laws governing it by citing earlier, universally accepted sources for support, and they insisted on compliance because of their rank and prestige among the people. These leaders did not teach out of conviction or by example, as Jesus does. Jesus says, "You have heard it said . . . But I tell you. . . ." Jesus lives what he teaches. His authority is self-generated. He also understands the limitations of unbending legalistic interpretations and allows for conscientious and prudent application when occasion demands. When Jesus speaks, people listen, instinctively realizing they are hearing objective truth warmed by compassionate understanding.

How does Jesus come by the assuredness he exhibits in teaching, given his humble background and lack of formal education? What's more, he departs so significantly from the usual legalism and imposition of ritual regulations that it is astonishing he has the courage to differ openly with the acknowledged authorities, even as his life is threatened for doing so.

5. Jesus Feeds the Multitudes

In the gospels we learn of two occasions in which Jesus feeds thousands who follow him. We also know how, through bread and wine, he devises an amazing way to remain with his disciples beyond death. Hospitality is a defining virtue among Semitic peoples. To provide others, especially strangers, with refreshment and shelter is to confer on them life itself. Jesus confers life, as hospitality demands of him, whether feeding his followers bread or his own body in the form of bread. Even beyond those signs and realities, his teaching and his cures produce life; his compassionate forgiveness welcomes sinners back into the open arms of a loving God.

Everything Jesus does is for the creation or enhancement of life.

How is it that Jesus' disciples so readily accept his eucharistic presence as a wildly imaginative means of remaining with them? Even more, how do they come to welcome this gift as his real presence, not simply as a symbolic reminder that he once walked among them?

*

Meditate on these mysteries. Let your imagination wander wherever the Spirit leads, and see if you do not feel more convinced of Jesus' mission on earth and your association with that mission in your time and place. Then see if you can identify further "wondrous" mysteries from other parts of Jesus' public life with which to fashion another more personal set for your own meditation. In Pope John Paul's "Mysteries of Light" on Jesus' public life, three of the five mysteries coincide at least partly with those proposed above. This pure coincidence illustrates the real possibility of your discerning for yourself which appropriately important gospel incidents you would find challenging to your spiritual growth as you pray the Rosary. With the encouragement you have now, what reason is there to hesitate any longer?

3

The Vocation Mysteries

Every person eventually finds somewhere to settle in the world, in society, and, to at least some degree, in a sense of self-fulfillment. That person has, it is said, found his or her "niche" or vocation in life.

Assuming, as do most exegetes, that Jesus only gradually—but surely—came to realize the totality of who he was and what his mission was on earth, I reflected that (as an adolescent and as a young man) he must have devoted considerable time to discerning his vocation. Being "one of us" by participating fully in the lot of humanity, it is not probable he enjoyed visions or other supernatural occurrences to initiate or confirm his choices in life. As do we in our circumstances, he came in time to where he "found" himself and became confident of his capabilities. This realization must have coincided closely with his baptism and his subsequent time in the desert.

It made sense to me, then, to consider collecting five circumstances, events, or encounters that would suggest Jesus prayed over his vocation in life before taking action. These were important moments during which Jesus came to a clearer conception of his identity and mission. After some thought, I surfaced the following:

Jesus Becomes Aware of a Call
Jesus Reflects in Response to the Call
Jesus Makes a Decision
Jesus Acts on His Decision
Jesus Repeatedly Reaffirms His
    Decision

I think it is easy enough to see the dynamic that comes into play under the rubric of such mysteries. Consider each briefly.

1. Jesus Becomes Aware of a Call

Jesus, sensing he has a special mission in life, takes a stance of openness and listening to God as to the nature of that mission. After his baptism, his lengthy retreat in the wilderness, and his return to live and preach among the people, especially the poor, he shows an awareness that he has been chosen and sent by God to undertake a very special mission in this world (Cf. Lk 4:18–21, et al).

2. Jesus Reflects in Response to the Call

Jesus considers his call seriously and prayerfully, and his Father responds by showing him in some manner the requirements and the challenging potential of his call before Jesus takes action. Perhaps Jesus now begins to think twice about what he discerns, as not all of it looms pleasantly despite the noble objective (Cf. Mt 16:21, Mk 8:34, et al).

3. Jesus Makes a Decision

It is necessary to reflect on all the elements that go into a decision, but at a given point the time comes to make the decision. Jesus, at last satisfied that he did have a special call from God his Father, after he had reflected adequately on the implications of that call, knew it was time to take a decision to act. He did so, courageously if also somewhat apprehensively (Cf. Lk 9:44, 51; Jn 11:7–15).

4. Jesus Acts on His Decision

Once he decides, Jesus wastes no time in taking action. The decision is one thing; setting it in motion is another, and, as he knew, there would be consequences, many of them undesirable. The same spirit of fortitude that prompted his decision also underlay his taking action in starting upon the mission he was convinced he had been called to fulfill (Cf. Jn 7:6–10).

5. Jesus Repeatedly Reaffirms His Decision

Early on, Jesus encounters such a puzzling mixture of responses to his message that he is compelled to continue praying over his decision, reflecting continuously on its relevance to the needs of the people, and reaffirming that the message is from God (Cf. Mk 1:35, Lk 5:16, Lk 6:12, Mk 6:5).

*

This Jesus-centered approach alone, I believe, justifies the *Vocation Mysteries*. Yet, there is another dimension that can provide beneficial opportunities for reflection. I refer to applying the substance of the mysteries to the pray-er.

In my own vocation in life, I too have been aware of each of the steps noted in the mysteries. I became aware at a certain time that I was attracted to the religious life as a brother. I, of course, took time to consider the rather sudden inclination I was experiencing (not having been especially drawn to it till then), testing it by time and reflection on the probable implications. When nothing deterred me, when all advice seemed fundamentally supportive, when the attraction grew even greater in intensity, I had to conclude I was not being misled, and I felt I must honor the call as I interpreted it.

But I had two years remaining in secondary school, and though I could transfer to the brothers' pre-novitiate academic program in another state to complete my schooling, relatives and I thought it prudent to continue where I was, participating in the activities of normal teenage life (including after-school work and social activities), and, if my call were as strongly felt when I completed my senior year, I would follow through. And that is what happened. I took action, applied, and, after acceptance, readied myself to leave home permanently.

The decision-making was, however, far from over. To number the times I had to confirm my choice over the following years would be impossible. The community authorities themselves had to rule on my acceptability and renew that decision officially several times until I was approved to make my profession of perpetual vows. Each stage of incorporation demanded that I myself renew my intention to remain in the brotherhood. Even after my perpetual vows, other events arose naturally as years passed that challenged me to renew my decision, to reconfirm the *yes* that was the original response to my call. As for most living their vocation, whatever it may be, that *yes* must be spoken over and over again through the years as a constant renewal of the vocational covenant between God and each person. God calls each of us to a special form of relationship that flows out of love into the service of others.

Whether one's vocation has been to the married state, to the priesthood, or to unmarried celibacy in or outside religious life, it is a call from God. Hopefully one's chosen profession is also prayerfully considered, so it also is a call from God. One's method of responding defines the nature of the eternal covenant existing between God and the one formed in God's image and likeness, called by name, and placed on earth at a particular time and place in a unique social and familial context, with a mission in life. God summons us to a covenant relationship, not to a particular task; our human proclivities lead us in one direction or another, but God works within all the human and natural elements that form the context in which we choose our life's work.

Using the Vocation Mysteries to pray the Rosary draws the individual into an area of reflection that facilitates both spiritual understanding and growth. It can be the occasion of the reaffirmation of God's call and an awareness of the courage God provides to "stay the course" throughout life. It can be the means to eventual union with God through the person's vocation to which the person, though responsible for the choice, has been invited and has faithfully responded.

Allow yourself to become immersed in the mystery underlying a call from God, both as it affected the human Jesus and as it has played itself out in your life. You may be amazed at the insights that reflecting on this set of circumstances prompts, though anything can and should be expected from a God of surprises.

4

The Golden Rule Mysteries

Christian or not, everyone is aware of "the golden rule" and observes it as conscience dictates: *Do to others as you would have them to do to you* (Lk 6:31).

The golden rule can be called plain old common sense as well as popular and Christian morality. Had Jesus never come as man among us, natural law and reasonable principles of ethics would at the very least have demanded of humanity this level of mutual respect and cooperation. If for no other reason than maintaining fundamentally benevolent relationships with others, we humans would have had to devise this "golden rule."

Jesus founded much of his teaching on already existing laws and traditions among the

Jewish people. Mixed in as they were with their Roman occupiers, the Jews felt in need of criteria by which relations could be judged as appropriate or not. If Jews and Romans were not exactly friends, they behaved for the most part in a civil way, tolerating each other out of necessity if nothing else, though in some cases there existed real respect.

Jesus, in his mission as an itinerant preacher proclaiming the presence of God's kingdom, seized on this common principle—the golden rule—and enlarged on it in several proverbial statements that carried the theme of the rule to its logical ends, particularly as applied specifically to various areas of behavior or relationship.

Taking Luke 6:36–38 as a starting point, I have classified five statements attributed to Jesus and summarized by the early Christian community as a portion of the so-called "Sermon on the Mount," and have highlighted their potential as five elements of Jesus' teaching that lend themselves conveniently and appropriately to reflection as accompaniment to the five decades of the Rosary.

The five *Golden Rule Mysteries* are:

Jesus teaches: "Be merciful, just as your Father is merciful" (Lk 6:36).

Jesus teaches: "Do not judge, and you
will not be judged" (Lk 6:37).

Jesus teaches: "Do not condemn, and
you will not be condemned" (Lk
6:37).

Jesus teaches: "Forgive, and you will be
forgiven" (Lk 6:37).

Jesus teaches: "Give, and it will be
given to you" (Lk 6:38a).

Jesus adds to the last a motivational
statement: "The measure you give will be the
measure you get back (Lk 6:38b)."

Jesus warns (Lk 6:32–33) against doing good
simply to invite similar behavior toward
yourself. What merit is there in that? Don't the
pagans do as much? How, then, do we—self-
proclaimed followers of Jesus—differ from non-
believers when we engage in this same type of
behavior? What is the crucial line of
demarcation?

Meditating on these five "mysteries," perhaps better called "Christian characteristics,"
provides a regular and substantial opportunity
to answer that question, even if only gradually
and imperfectly.

Let us consider each statement briefly.

1. Jesus teaches: "Be merciful, just as your Father is merciful."

For the word *merciful*, the Jerusalem Bible substitutes *compassionate*, not an earth-shaking replacement, but one that suggests we think more deeply about the intent of this command. Whichever of the two words attracts us, the meaning is clear enough. We are expected to exercise the primary characteristic by which Christians know and name God. We are to be God-like, not as remarkable or unreasonable an expectation as it sounds, for we are made "in God's image, and in God's likeness we were created" (Gn 1:26). Why, then, should we not be merciful or exercise compassion? Circumstances naturally evoke such a response from us if we have any sensitivity at all. Why should it be any different if we situate that response in a consciously loving context?

2. Jesus teaches: "Do not judge, and you will not be judged."

It doesn't take much for us to absorb the meaning of this statement. In fact, like the following mandate, it has a hint of a threat attached to it. If we judge others, for whatever reason, we ourselves are liable to judgment. Because it is Jesus who speaks, we assume it is God who will judge us if we judge others. Possibly so, though it is far more likely—even logical—we will judge ourselves, and do so on the basis of the very criteria we have used to judge others. That can be an uncomfortable thought, particularly if we know we have been less than sympathetic or entirely balanced and unbiased in our judgment of the actions, decisions, idiosyncrasies, or methods of others.

The tendency to be judgmental is one of the strongest and most common among us. Reflecting on this mystery as we pray a decade of the Rosary will help us maintain an awareness of our inclination along this line.

3. Jesus teaches: "Do not condemn, and you will not be condemned."

This statement sounds quite similar to the previous one. But think of both the practical act of judging, then condemning, and of the attitudinal mind-set associated with the two actions, and the distinctions seem to take on a more concrete shape.

In any case, condemnation implies one specific and conclusive judgment, not a whole range of potential or intermediate judgments. To avoid condemning someone, whatever the reason, we must avoid being judgmental, because condemnation tends to follow judgment.

4. Jesus teaches: "Forgive, and you will be forgiven."

The second and third mysteries in this set are expressed negatively: do *not* do this and it will *not* be done to you. The direction returns now to the positive with the fourth consideration, forgiveness.

We often hear victims of criminal acts say that they can never forget what has happened to them; they will (or will not) be able to forgive the perpetrator. We ourselves make every effort to forgive relatives, friends, and others when they have somehow trodden on our rights, sensitivities, intentions, or preferences. The question we must always pose regarding this characteristic is: what *is* true forgiveness, and do I have it within me fully and honestly to forgive? Is it not true that, in our attempt at forgiving, we may, consciously or unconsciously, withhold a small corner of our total forgiveness, perhaps reserving it as a weapon with which to engage later in another stage of self-serving negotiation in our relationship with the person we are forgiving?

True forgiveness is not easy to summon from the depths of our hurt. For that reason we need to reflect on these words of Jesus and consider how gradually we may become not only more conscious of our practice of forgiveness, but better able to exercise it in ever greater increments.

5. Jesus teaches: "Give, and it will be given to you."

Few, if any, have exemplified the virtue of generosity, of freely giving, as did Jesus. He gave not only of his giftedness, especially with his teaching and miraculous interventions, but of himself, "to the point of death—even to death on a cross" (Phil 2:8). This statement encourages us also to be generous in giving of who and what we are and have without fearing we will lack the necessities of life ourselves. This mandate may strike many of us more at the core of our being than the other mysteries, because it applies directly to both personal and material possessions and our habitual relationship to them. If we are uneasy over possibly losing what we have, if we are inclined toward amassing the goods of this world, our attitude will interfere considerably with our ability to develop this teaching of Jesus, and we too, like the young man in the gospel (see Mt 19:16–22), will go away sad because we have many possessions.

We obviously do not function on a daily basis out of a bartering mode—giving only if being given to, offering only if we anticipate receiving something in return. But reflecting on this golden rule statement of Jesus when reciting these mysteries will give us an opportunity regularly to renew our determination to be generous out of a desire to be detached from those things that hinder a more perfect relationship with our God.

*

The implication in each of these five Semitic-style proverbs is that we must be or do as each advises because to do so is to act as God does.

Such is the manner in which these mandates relate directly to God: "You shall love the Lord your God with all your heart, and with all your soul, and with all your mind." Such also is the way these mandates relate to others: "You shall love your neighbor as yourself" (see Mt 22:34–40, Mk 12:28–33; and Lk 10:25–28).

Jesus suggests in Luke that acting as mandated will result in the establishment and/or enhancement of the proper relationship between God and the individual, and between one individual and another. "The measure you give will be the measure you get back"(Lk 6:38). It is clear that *mercy, judgment, condemnation, forgiveness,* and *generosity* imply a mutuality, a reciprocal exchange of graced energy, and that to be or do one of these characteristics automatically sets in motion a response in kind, whether on the part of God or of neighbor—or of both. These mandates do not spring from self-interest or a type of spiritual self-defense system, but from pristine motivation out of loving obedience to the Word of God.

Reflecting on this set of related gospel mandates can clarify and affirm for us the mystery of God's initial and ongoing intervention in creation through the incredible munificence of God's love and the implications logically following from the relationships that love enables. How does Mary exemplify the munificence of God's love? How can we include her in our reflection on the Golden Rule Mysteries?

This mix of affirmative and negative statements serves to remind us who pray the Rosary while reflecting on them that responding to these mysteries or characteristics is not optional, and how we do so will color our expectations of the response, be it human or divine.

How and why, we can ask, are we to be or not to be *compassionate, judgmental, condemning, forgiving*, and *generous*? That is the substance of what we meditate or reflect upon while praying the Rosary, and we do so in the light of the entirety of the gospel content and message, indeed, of all scripture, God's covenant with humankind.

This set of mysteries naturally connects with earlier ones, because in giving wholeheartedly, we are also being nonjudgmental, are being merciful, are not condemning, and are forgiving. To fulfill each of these mandates perfectly is the goal of a lifetime. Realistically, we may never achieve that goal, but progress should be discernible along the way.

5

The Rites of Passage
Mysteries

All of us can identify crucial moments or periods in life that signaled a watershed experience leading to irreversible change. We matured, perhaps suddenly; we were never the same again. Something major had occurred to contribute memorably to our fully human development, whatever our vocation in life summoned us to be. I suggest here five stages of potential challenge toward growth. They are only specific enough for you to recognize something from your own life experience that most closely fits these stages. The word *mystery* may once again be seen to refer more to an *event* or an *occasion* than to something unexplainable, yet there always exists at any notable time of growth the mysterious but loving hand of God present and active.

We know from our study and experience of culture what *rites of passage* are. We may be surprised to learn that, whether or not formal ceremonies were part of our maturation process, we did undergo in our physical, intellectual, emotional, social, and spiritual development clearly defined turning points or rites of passage following which we were, happily, never the same.

Let us begin by enumerating five possible stages of maturation that, if personalized, can provide you with five very appropriate moments of growth on which you can reflect in the context of the Rosary as prayer. Then, by way of an example to build upon, I will list and elaborate somewhat on five specific rites of passage I experienced and reveal why they influenced my life.

Five *Rites of Passage Mysteries* are:

To experience a major transition
    because of a memorable event in
    youth

To be influenced positively and
    permanently by another

> To respond to a surprising and
> transfiguring spiritual experience
> To experience the true meaning of life
> and death
> To become fully aware of one's unique
> giftedness

Even these, obviously, can allow for substitutions of occasions that, in your experience and judgment, are more appropriate for your reflective prayer at a given time in your life.

Here are five of my personal experiences:

1. I Respond to a Meaningful Academic Challenge

For whatever the reason—I was finally age-ready, my teachers were especially adept at their craft, or I was under family and peer pressure—for the first time in my schooling—early in my Junior year—I was confronted, singled out, challenged, prodded, and encouraged by two of my high school teachers. They demanded I discover and test my intellectual potential through my studies and that I pursue that potential productively. Neither considered mediocrity acceptable. Once I learned that these men would hound me until I produced what they apparently could see in me, I felt affirmed. Affirmation was an essential element in this *rite of passage*, and, once I acknowledged that these teachers might be right, I entered wholeheartedly into the process. For one class, that meant doing a book report on some literary classic each week instead of every six weeks, as was the standard for my classmates.

The flowing together of elements enabling this major turning point in my life undoubtedly arose from several sources. Whatever the cause, the realization that I was launching willingly and enthusiastically into an area previously unexplored served as motivation from that point on in my intellectual life, and unquestionably impacted other areas as well.

2. I Adapt to Nearly Any Environmental Circumstances

Only in hindsight do we draw solid conclusions from incidents in our lives that surround a particular theme. At some point I became aware that, in whatever circumstances I found myself—moving to another home, welcoming another baby brother into the family, living through the realities of wartime rationing, leaving home permanently to enter religious life—I was able to adapt with astonishing ease. For someone who became painfully homesick just staying overnight with a playmate at his family cottage twenty miles from home, how would it be possible that I could excitedly and permanently take leave of my home in pursuit of a vocation to religious life? Why was the resulting homesickness, though no different from earlier episodes, not strong enough to lure me back home? How was I able to encounter and accept whatever changes were imposed during the early years of being formed as a religious, especially when I changed houses seven times in as many years? How could I adapt from family life to living among dozens of individuals of similar age and intent? How could I feel comfortable almost immediately in whatever assignment I was given, whether to study a subject I knew little about, to become director of a residential boys' home, to move to Africa, to undertake major roles in community government, or to write a book without an unusually graced sense of God's presence and power in adapting at every step?

3. I Participate in a Significant Renewal Program

After twenty-five years as a religious, I asked to enroll in a spiritual renewal program—

"Sangre"—as part of a home sabbatical during a break from my years in Africa. The site was the desert mountains of New Mexico, the context an all-brothers' community made up of staff and twenty-eight participants from various congregations making the program, the duration of which was exactly one hundred days. This program was, in my judgment, the most critical turning point in my life. It was here that I began to accept myself without reservation and to learn I could generate confidence in myself and do whatever I was asked or desired to do. Without Sangre, I would never have had the courage or the capacity to undertake leadership roles in the congregation to which I belong. From this *refounding* program I emerged almost literally a new man, and the hundred-day experience has in some concrete way colored each of my days since.

4. I Value Challenging Experiences Gained by Serving in Community Government

I was elected "out of Africa" to head one of our congregation's provinces for a term of six years. It was both heart- and body-wrenching after thirteen years in Ghana to make such an abrupt change from African classroom to

American administration, but again the "mystery" of adaptability came into play. While provincial superior, I had both the need and opportunity to become familiar with the other sectors of the congregation, so I traveled to several continents for meetings. This exposure gave me a much wider perspective of Holy Cross than I had had, even with overseas experience.

Finishing my term, I engaged for some months in administrative work at Notre Dame for our missions until our general assembly elected me to a six-year term as assistant to the superior general, based in Rome. Again a great deal of travel was called for, and I added new dimensions as well as countries to my experience of Holy Cross.

The result of my holding these two positions, together with my prior roles as a religious superior in Africa and the United States, afforded me an unusually comprehensive knowledge of the congregation and an inside view of it from the legislative and executive standpoint, enabling me to consider this a major *rite of passage* in my life as a religious of Holy Cross.

5. I Benefit From Opportunities I Am Given to Write

Six months before I completed my tour of duty in Rome, my provincial asked me if I would be ready to do some writing to help the Brothers formally and officially commemorate the 175th anniversary of their founding in 1820 by Fr. James Dujarié. I was both honored and intrigued by the invitation, and, having been required to do a substantial amount of writing, translating, and editing while in Rome, I accepted the task of writing a biography of the first Holy Cross brother provincial in the United States, Br. Ephrem O'Dwyer. As I have often remarked since, had I known what the project would require in terms of time, energy, and disciplined perseverance, I would probably have argued. As it happened, I was blessed. The book was completed and published in plenty of time for the celebration.

Subsequently I was asked to handle the province newsletter. I also authored two short community histories, and I began writing articles—most of them on the Brotherhood—either for our newsletter or for a national periodical. I learned from the book experience that I had it within me to undertake a major writing project and carry it through. I also came to realize that writing was something I had always been relatively good at, wanted to do, and hoped to continue more or less regularly.

This discovery was perhaps for me the final *rite of passage* on the professional level, though God has ways of springing surprises not even the most fertile imaginations can fashion. It was one more example of critical crossroads in my life that led to irreversible changes in direction for me—to my benefit every time.

*

All of us can undertake similar prayerful reflection on our life passages by choosing five occasions of personally significant transition that resemble those given above. Meditating on them while praying the Rosary, we can benefit from our memories about times when we were acutely aware of God's presence and activity in our lives. We can even benefit from remembering occasions when we were not conscious that God was at work in us. The nature of the passages need not revolve around challenges from outside sources, but may well include self-generated challenges resulting from realizations or gained from prayer, spiritual direction, relationships, study, and other sources.

While praying these mysteries, we may at times want to go beyond our own experience and reflect on Jesus as one of us, as needing to encounter and negotiate passages in his life, and how in the gospel we see he accomplished this properly human task. We could even choose five events in the gospels that would equate as *rites of passage* for Jesus, God-with-us. We could also consider Mary's role in her son's passages: co-responsible, as at the wedding at Cana, or an observer, as when she followed her son and witnessed his highly effective preaching. It doesn't take great imagination to picture Jesus experiencing five crossroads that arguably contributed significantly to his human development. I suggest a few here, but your participation in the hunt through the gospels will augment your desire to utilize this set of mysteries to reflect on your own *rites of passage* and their impact on your life, and then perhaps make a humble comparison with those of Jesus you uncover.

Think of the following as possibilities: the wedding at Cana, the rejection of Jesus by his townsfolk in the synagogue, his baptism and the retreat that followed, the transfiguration, and the agony in the garden. Each seems to be an experience of irreversible impact in Jesus' life. Use these and more to formulate your own set of Rites of Passage Mysteries involving Jesus. The result can be nothing less than an eye-opening experience for you as you pray the Rosary.

In whatever way you decide to use crucial points of growth in your life, the field is broad and beckoning, as all of us travel the same ground repeatedly. Praying the Rosary while meditating on such events can assure you of benefiting significantly from this wholesome process.

6

The Hidden Life Mysteries

After relating the infancy narrative, the author of Luke is silent regarding the life of Jesus at his home in Nazareth with Joseph and Mary until the incident of the boy's remaining in the Temple in Jerusalem at the end of the family's pilgrimage.

We are told that his parents found him talking with Jewish teachers in the Temple. Despite Jesus' plea that he must be doing what God asked of him, he acceded to his parents' wishes and went back to Nazareth where he was an obedient son to them.

"And he was subject to them" is a description that leaves unanswered almost every question we might pose about the childhood, adolescence, and youth of Jesus. If we are curious about the development of our savior as one sharing our humanity, our wonder must include his early years as well as those chronicled in the gospels.

The Wondrous mysteries, added to the traditional Glorious, Joyful, and Sorrowful ones, help our prayerful reflection on Jesus' infancy, passion, death, and resurrection, as well as elements characteristic of his public life.

To compensate for the silence surrounding the other years of Jesus' life, I have selected five realities Jesus surely experienced in some very human way. I have set them in the reflective format of the Rosary, calling them the *Hidden Life Mysteries.*

The Hidden Life Mysteries are:

Jesus, Citizen of Nazareth

Jesus the Teenager

Jesus and the World of Work

Jesus Assumes Household
     Responsibilities

Jesus Begins in Prayer to Discern the
     Father's Call

What can be said about each of these areas of Jesus' early life?

1. Jesus, Citizen of Nazareth

I envision Jesus as a small child playing with friends on the dusty streets of Nazareth, as an older child engaging in boys' games, as an adolescent preparing for his *bar mitzvah*, and as a young man spending an evening in friendly conversation with neighborhood youth. I am struck by the awesome implications of the Incarnation, that is, God's becoming a human being like us in every aspect except the disorder that results in estrangement from God. Certainly a mystery of profound depth lies beneath the process by which Jesus became aware of the consequences of who he was and, more importantly, what was to be his role among us in the context of a particular time and place in the course of human history. I might reflect on a Watergate-type question: "What did Jesus know about his divinity, and when did he know it?" Whatever the answer, for all those early years he was an unpretentious citizen of his home town. What does his identity as an ordinary citizen say to me about Jesus? What does it say to me about my responsibilities as a member of the microcosm of human society I inhabit and influence?

2. Jesus the Teenager

No one will have difficulty imagining what topics could be drawn into this reflection. Just recalling my own teenage years is revealing enough. We get a hint of what maturing meant in Jesus' staying behind in Jerusalem and, when found, his rather curt response to his mother's question. If Jesus was beginning to discern in prayer with his Father what his vocation was to be, the child would sense his growing autonomy and be short with his parents. What teenager would not be? What did facing adulthood mean to Jesus? With what "rules" in Mary and Joseph's house did Jesus have problems, thinking them too controlling, too constraining, too childish, too directive as he grew older? Where did he let his imagination roam, and where were his dreams? How did he view the expectation that he take over the family business rather than strike out on his own? How did his status in Jewish tradition as an only child impact his expectations for the future?

3. Jesus and the World of Work

It became obvious early in Jesus' life that, coming from a poor craftsman's family, he would be expected to learn the various elements of his father's trade and contribute his part to the support of the family. He would have been reminded as he grew that he must become the carpenter or craftsman his father was, and would have been at least unofficially apprenticed to Joseph. Lacking any indication of when Joseph died, we are left to entertain two possibilities: either the death occurred when Jesus was quite young, though after he had been trained in his father's trade; or, Jesus worked side by side with Joseph for years, perhaps under the shingle of "Yusef and Yeshua Ben Yusef, Craftsmen." In either case, Jesus was introduced early to the reality and expectations of the world of work and the responsibilities it inevitably entailed.

4. Jesus Assumes Household Responsibilities

Work was but one responsibility. What else would Jesus have been expected to undertake as duties both when a child and as he grew into young manhood? If Joseph died early on, naturally Jesus would be responsible for taking over the entirety of the business: soliciting orders, executing them, stocking materials, calculating prices, keeping books, occasionally hiring part time assistants, competing honestly, observing fair sales practices, and so on. He would have been aware of outside influences on business, such as Rome's impact on the local economy through taxation. He would of necessity have been the initiator and leader of religious practices and be responsible for observing all essential rubrics in the home, and would have taken his place in the synagogue, perhaps even attended a yeshiva for a time. He would have been aware of his mother's expectations as a widow and of his responsibility to her. He would have been conscious of social obligations in a small Jewish village, including the likely expectation that he marry.

5. Jesus Begins in Prayer to Discern the Father's Call

A persisting question among scholars is, "When did Jesus know with certainty that he was God?" Assumptions that he was always fully conscious of his nature as God as well as human have largely been dismissed as not reflecting the reality of what it would have meant to be *fully* human. If he had always realized he was God, that would have influenced every aspect of his humanity. He could not have gone through the trials of growing and developing as truly one of us if a perpetually valid "get out of jail free" card was included in his Monopoly for Life game. There is no doubt he came to be convinced of his identity at a given point, but no indication exists that it had to have been while he was a small child, even a youth "about his father's business." This is the mystery of the two natures of Jesus, and no amount of speculation will supply us this side of heaven with an adequate explanation.

We ourselves know well the meaning of being human and can reflect to advantage on that aspect of Jesus' life. It is likely it was in prayer that the relationship of Jesus to God began to become clearer and clearer to him, leading to his sensing a call to announce by word and deed to a waiting people that the end time was now, that God was indeed with them in Jesus, and he would always be with them through his Spirit. Was it this realization that eventually called him to sever ties with his mother and leave home to become the itinerant preacher his mission obviously summoned him to be?

*

Now, these five mysteries admittedly comprise significant circumstances typical of anyone's early years. Yet, there are still other possibilities. You may surface several more yourself, and why not? Let the imagination roam freely between the lines of the gospel accounts and see what emerges. In the meantime, these mysteries should serve to set in motion your praying the Rosary in this context.

These Hidden Life Mysteries focus on Jesus, Mary, and Joseph and call you to place yourself in the period of time actually lived by God-with-us, Emmanuel, some two thousand years ago. What prevents your glancing back on your own childhood, adolescence, and youth and recalling those graced moments, events, and periods that contributed to your maturing into an awareness of God's presence, open to the consequences of that presence? What do you recall that significantly contributed to your developing from childhood into adolescence? How did you negotiate the important passage toward increasing independence as a unique personality? It seems almost irreverent to imagine Jesus would have encountered the very same crises as are typical of our development, but he did. Reflecting on that astonishing reality in prayer can invite and encourage us to be open to an awareness of the closeness of our God to us through the very same Spirit of Jesus who animated his own hidden but growth-filled years.

7

Mysteries of the Psalter

A nyone who uses the Psalms as prayer knows the appeal of certain verses. The sentiments found there seem at times to reflect the experience of the one praying in an especially relevant way.

The Psalms may be part of one's daily prayer, as they are for the clergy, religious, and lay persons who regularly recite portions of the Liturgy of the Hours. Psalms may be chosen at random for private prayer. The ancient and inspired wisdom born of experience resonates with everyone to some degree and potentially becomes one's own personal prayer.

We are probably more familiar with oft-quoted verses from the Psalms than we realize. If we made a purposeful search through the 150 prayers, songs, or poems, I believe we would be surprised at our familiarity with far more than, "The Lord is my Shepherd."

In this chapter I show from my experience how your personal use of the Psalter can be organized according to your choice of themes for adaptation to reflections meant to accompany the Rosary. The Psalms are in themselves exceptionally rich in prayerful expression. How excerpts can be so conveniently fitted to both a theme and to groupings of five is not astonishing because of the endless potential for prayer contained within them.

I have gathered four sets of *Psalter Mysteries* here: those that are focused on the contemplative side of one's prayer; those expressing a close relationship between the one praying and God to whom the prayer is addressed; those that dwell on specific personal themes; and those stressing one's habitual stance of waiting and watching patiently for God in one's life.

Of course, anyone can create several sets of mysteries to accompany a reflective praying of the Rosary. What are your favorite passages, and what themes do they suggest? To begin, pick five that are particularly familiar and try reflecting on them as your fingers slip over the beads. The following sets represent passages that, over the years, have proved especially appropriate to the unfolding of my own life and they are offered here primarily as examples for you.

How do I use these verses for reflection as I pray the Rosary? Briefly, as follows:

The Psalter Mysteries I (Contemplative)

Psalm 27:4
Psalm 27:8–9
Psalm 42:2
Psalm 46:10
Psalm 84:1–2

1. Psalm 27:4

One thing I asked of the Lord, that will I seek after:
to live in the house of the Lord all the days of my life,
to behold the beauty of the Lord, and to inquire in his temple.

I think it is obvious the psalmist is not expressing a longing to live out his days literally in the confines of the magnificent Temple in Jerusalem. David—or whoever is originally responsible for the wording—has visited the Temple, perhaps many times, and has found there for himself a peace not available elsewhere, a sense of God's presence and power among humans. The peacefulness has served as a preview of the eternal peace and divine presence to come in the next life and inspires the psalmist to yearn for the perfection and preservation of the consoling experience on which he bases his words.

We can compare this longing to our own. We seek God habitually and try to allow no other attraction to conflict with our longing for all those elements of life we associate with beauty and with the constant dialogue that constitutes the uninterrupted face-to-face search to know the essence of God in the beatific vision.

2. Psalm 27:8–9

"Come," my heart says, "seek his face!"
   Your face, Lord, do I seek.
Do not hide your face from me.

One of the deepest longings provoked by love is for the continuous presence of the beloved. This verse, part of the same contemplative urge found in verse four of the same psalm, personifies the heart of the one praying as addressing the whole person, stirring up the desire to contemplate the face of God, that is, God as God. A response concludes the dialogue: of course he or she is searching for God, and begs God not to withdraw or remain hidden.

This prayer implies that presence is enough for us. Finding God is at the heart of our deepest longing. A fitting interpretation of this verse is Augustine's assertion that our hearts are restless and will not be satisfied until they have found their rest in God. We may not consider ourselves contemplatives; in fact, few of us are. But all of us have a contemplative side to our spiritual selves that demands to be nourished by the only Food of Life that can fill us. Words are unnecessary in contemplative prayer: it is the silent longing of the heart for God.

3. Psalm 42:2

My soul thirsts for God, for the living God.
When shall I come and behold the face of God?

The heart thirsts for the water of life that only God can offer. In a near-agony of spiritual longing, the soul asks rhetorically when it will at last realize the object of its search, attaining the presence of the living God. The earlier analogy of the deer longing for water sketches a clear image of the extent of the thirst experienced by the soul. Some translations read, "As the deer pants for a running stream. . . ," illustrating the breathless urgency of the search for God. Words fail the one praying; only God's presence will satisfy the persistent longing.

Again, meager as may be our awareness of the contemplative side of our soul, it is there and will be heard if we are in the least attentive to our spiritual journey and the ways of God, who draws us along the path leading at last to discovery. Allowing ourselves to relax into a quiet sense of wordless seeking may result in more from our recitation of the repetitive prayers of the Rosary than any conscious pursuit of the meaning of the words we employ either in the quotation from the psalms or the Hail Mary we say over and over.

4. Psalm 46:10

"Be still, and know that I am God."

This brief passage is one of the most powerful and meaningful of the entire Psalter, indeed, of all scripture. For every question, for every difficulty we encounter, for every unresolved conflict, for every apparently impossible task we are obliged to accomplish, God is there. This quotation takes the form of God speaking to us rather than of our addressing God. God suggests we should abandon things that clutter our minds and hearts and simply listen in absolute interior silence, because God speaks in equally silent but perfectly effective ways to us when we adopt the posture of humble listening and readiness. When God speaks, things happen.

This verse is a prayer we may use to advantage many times a day even with no reference to the Rosary. But it is particularly powerful as one of the mysteries of God's covenant with humanity when we dwell on the passage in the context of the rest of our mysteries that, taken as a whole, draw our minds and hearts to the divine object of our contemplation.

5. Psalm 84:1–2

How lovely is your dwelling place,
O Lord of hosts!
My soul longs, indeed it faints for the courts of
*   the Lord.*

This passage sums up the continuous longing for God felt in the heart of the one praying, once again using the Jerusalem temple as symbolic of God's presence to the entire Jewish people as well as to the individual worshiper. The psalmist and those using this prayer as their own reiterate the sentiments of Psalm 27, but this verse expresses an increase in the intensity of the soul's longing to dwell forever in the courts of the Lord, a home lovely beyond compare.

We are aware that each psalm is the work of an individual who experienced whatever it was that inspired the substance of the poetic prayer; yet, we are also invited by the church to utilize these psalms as our personal prayer, and they have been adopted as an official expression of the longing of the church in its Liturgy of the Hours and in the celebration of every Eucharistic sacrifice. How the psalms will be of use to us individually depends on how relevant we believe them to be to our life experiences, both past and present. Because experience is ongoing, so is the potential for the application of the depths of meaning of the various psalms to our situation. A psalm that seems today to have no bearing on our life may tomorrow be the very prayer that most effectively expresses precisely what our hearts are most desirous of saying to God.

*

Having established the value of the psalms as prayer and of poignant verses excerpted from them as subjects for reflection during our recitation of the Rosary, I will list three more sets of Psalter Mysteries here and include the verse, but will refrain from going into the same detailed commentary accorded the first set, presuming you will be anxious to pursue your own search for favorite passages and will gather five of them into a meaningful collection that will serve as a personal set of Psalter Mysteries inspired by your own rationale. In the meantime, my experience of these particular passages perhaps will be a springboard from which you can launch into more personally meaningful selections.

The Psalter Mysteries II (Relational)

These verses from another set of psalms are more directly tied to a sense of the relationship existing between a soul and God. This relationship is otherwise known as the *spirituality* proper to an individual. The second mystery here might well have been included among the selections for the contemplative set, but it is equally fitting as an expression of one's belonging to and being in constant search of God.

1. Psalm 23:4

> *Even though I walk through the darkest valley,*
> *I fear no evil; for you are with me.*

2. Psalm 63:1

> *O God, you are my God, I seek you,*
> *my flesh faints for you; my soul thirsts for you;*
> *as in a dry and weary land where there is no water.*

3. Psalm 84:6

> *As they go through the valley of Baca*
> *they make it a place of springs.*

4. Psalm 100:3

> *Know that the Lord is God.*
> *It is he that made us, and we are his;*
> *we are his people, and the sheep of his pasture.*

5. Psalm 119:176

I have gone astray like a lost sheep; seek out your
servant.

The Psalter Mysteries III (Personal)

These verses constitute a series of mysteries more illustrative of a very personal connection between God as parent and the individual praying out of a stance as a child of God. The concept of "fear of God" appears in two selections. It is, of course, understood that fear bears no connection to "being afraid of God." Fear in the biblical sense is a humble acknowledgment of right relationships, it is filial piety, it is walking confidently toward the God who walks always welcomingly toward you. In the third mystery, think of *house* more as the sum and substance of your life.

1. Psalm 103:11

For as the heavens are high above the earth,
so great is his steadfast love toward those who
fear him.

2. Psalm 103:13

As a father has compassion for his children,
so the Lord has compassion for those who fear
*   him.*

3. Psalm 127:1

Unless the Lord builds the house,
those who build it labor in vain.

4. Psalm 139:14

I praise you, for I am fearfully and wonderfully
*   made.*
Wonderful are your works;
that I know very well.

5. Psalm 149:4

For the Lord takes pleasure in his people;
he adorns the humble with victory.

The Psalter Mysteries IV (Watching and Waiting)

These mysteries center around verses that speak of the soul's readiness for God's coming into its life, of patient openness to God's appearance when and in the manner that best fits God's plan. If we consider the amount of time we spend waiting and watching for people and events, not to mention answers to prayer, we gain an added appreciation of the meaning of those realities when related to the soul's ongoing longing for God. This awareness is at the heart of contemplative prayer.

1. Psalm 25:5

You are the God of my salvation;
for you I wait all day long.

2. Psalm 27:14

Be strong and let your heart take courage;
wait for the Lord!

3. Psalm 37:7

Be still before the Lord, and wait patiently for him.

4. Psalm 62:1

For God alone my soul waits in silence;
from him comes my salvation.

5. Psalm 130:5-6

*I wait for the Lord, my soul waits, and in his
word I hope;*
*my soul waits for the Lord more than those who
watch for the morning.*

*

Whether you prefer using one of these sets of mysteries taken from verses of various psalms, or selecting your own favorite passages from among the 150 rich and beautiful prayers of the Old Testament, I encourage you to immerse yourself in the depths of meaning and the astonishing relevance of the psalms as personal prayer, prayer fit to accompany the recitation of the Rosary. The benefit of reflecting on such elements as the contemplative expression of our prayer, the relationship existing between God and us, the personal love shown, parent-like, by God for each of us, and our being ready and aware of God's coming into our lives—none of those can be stressed too strongly. The proven "track record" the psalms enjoy as long-standing prayers of the universal church is enough to recommend their inclusion in our regular prayer. The logical ease with which they lend themselves, as single verses, to a meditative praying of the Rosary is additional encouragement to make them often a part of our prayer.

8

The Wit and Wisdom
Mysteries

The *Wit and Wisdom Mysteries* illustrate Jesus'
capacity to confound, astonish, or educate
by means of his sharp wit or evident wisdom
those with whom he engages in dialogue.

You, like I, have come across incidents in the
gospels in which it appears Jesus is being
treated badly, being taken advantage of by what
seem to be superior intellects—and surely
superior posturing—of the Jewish leaders. Yet,
nearly always Jesus emerges the clear winner
and our hearts are excited by the manner in
which he does it. And were there not times we
smiled, appreciating his cleverness? Often it is
through a play on words the irony of a
situation that we see how competent Jesus was

in matching wits and in plumbing the depths of both natural and divine wisdom to address the situation at hand. Why should we not once in a while use examples of this talent as the substance of our reflection as we pray the Rosary?

Of all incidents possible in this category, I have selected five from the gospels that show an approach Jesus often took in conversation with his listeners or questioners. Meditating on such events in the context of the Rosary is an alternative method of praying the five decades that offers us an opportunity to image Jesus more vividly in our mind and heart and to appreciate the ongoing mystery of how this poor, largely uneducated craftsman evolved into such an authoritative teacher.

Remember, these are but five of the many examples that could be highlighted from the pages of the gospels. Your own spirituality and preferences will suggest others with which you more closely identify.

These are the Wit and Wisdom Mysteries:
Jesus makes clever use of parables to spread his message (Cf. Lk 10:30 *ff*, Lk 15:11 *ff*, etc.)

Jesus shows wit in dialogue with the
    Samaritan and Syro-Phoenician
    women (Jn 4:1 *ff*, Mt 15:11 *ff*)
Jesus confounds the accusers of the
    woman taken in adultery (Jn 8:2–11)
Jesus rains confusion on those who
    question his authority (Cf. Jn 7)
Jesus teaches a practical lesson to the
    Emmaus disciples (Lk 24:13 *ff*)

These titles could be less lengthy, but when more descriptive they have greater impact. A closer investigation of each of these five situations will help you see, with your own careful reading of the gospels, what you might surface as similar events that for you take on even greater appropriateness in this category of mysteries.

1. Jesus Makes Clever Use of Parables to Spread His Message

There are forty parables in the Synoptic gospels alone. The authors of these anecdotal tales selected representative examples to appeal to the illiterate among the early Christians and to show how strong a grasp Jesus had on psychology, folklore, pedagogy, and theological and cultural traditions. Add to those his surprising capability to engage both wit and wisdom in relating these brief tales and applying their meaning appropriately.

For myself, I can reflect on my understanding of scripture and my opportunities to influence others by the spoken word—be it by informal conversation, teaching, or oratory. I can also ask myself how I am influenced by the One who, through these parables, speaks to me just as surely as he spoke to his disciples or the crowds that gathered to listen to him. All of us need to ask the same questions about how we influence others, and the extent to which we allow ourselves to be impacted by Jesus' teachings.

2. Jesus Shows Wit in Dialogue With the Samaritan and Syro-Phoenician Women

Jesus broke local custom when he conversed with the Samaritan woman about Messianic expectations and about living water. He appeared to be almost cruel in his treatment of the Caananite woman from the district of Tyre and Sidon who begged Jesus to drive a demon out of her daughter. In both cases, Jesus appears to show disrespect, even to hurl an insult. He catches the Samaritan woman in a lie about her marital status, and with cushioned wit chides her. The Syro-Phoenician woman seems to exhibit sharper wit than Jesus, but he appreciates her riposte and praises her bold confidence. In the end, he is impressed by the evident faith and humility of each woman and he responds with compassion.

I see in these confrontations the agility of Jesus' human intellect and the sentiment residing in his heart. I take comfort knowing that however impossible my needs and requests may seem, the One about whom I meditate in these passages is the God who has power to engage whatever is at enmity within me and be the eventual victor. I see that faith, confidence, and perseverance impress and move Jesus and have an effect on the outcome of the conversation. What prevents me—or you— from approaching him more consciously in a similar way?

3. Jesus Confounds the Accusers of the Woman Taken in Adultery

This confrontation between Jesus and the Jewish leaders is one of the most satisfying encounters chronicled in the gospels. Jesus' restrained, diplomatic, and marvelously effective manner of dealing with an obvious attempt to entrap him and make him look foolish is food for serious reflection. His separate but related conversation with the woman is one of the great examples of mercy and compassion, joining with justice to provide a realistic but humane and hope-filled outcome.

I know more than one method by which I can meditate on this event and contemplate the mysterious ways of God among humans. The first is simply to review the circumstances of the occasion and be awed by Jesus' wisdom. Another is to place myself in the scene in some way—as a silent bystander, as one of the participants in the dialogue, as the man with whom the woman was caught but who seems to have gotten away scot free, or maybe as a supposedly impartial human judge interpreting the Jewish law. In any case, I have to be impressed, and I come away content that Jesus has prevailed in spite of organized opposition.

4. Jesus Rains Confusion on Those Who Question His Authority

Because of his unimpressive origins and the way he boldly skirts about the flanks of traditional Jewish authority, Jesus is regarded as an upstart, a meddler, even an imposter. He would likely have been ignored had it not been for the influence his words and works had among the people. Threatened with irrelevance and impotence, the Jewish leaders fought back, trying to embarrass Jesus whenever the opportunity arose. The results, however, habitually ended with the embarrassment hurled back into their own faces, as in the incident proposed here for reflection.

I can meditate on the confidence of the One in whom I place my entire trust in matters that confuse and challenge me. I can recall that this same Jesus, not one bit different now than when he faced those leaders, will be my champion when I too am confronted by circumstances that aim to derail my efforts at ongoing conversion. Or, I may simply stand and stare in awe at the inherent authority residing in the strength of Jesus' personality that enables him to confront the legalistic power exerted against him.

5. Jesus Teaches a Practical Lesson to the Emmaus Disciples

This passage is a favorite of many who meditate on scripture. Jesus, after his resurrection, pretends to be a stranger and "by coincidence" finds himself on foot traveling to Emmaus, where two of the disciples are returning after the crucifixion. They are, understandably, discouraged and without hope, for they have concluded that Jesus was after all not what he made himself out to be, or even what his disciples were convinced he was. Jesus uses the long walk to re-educate them and leaves them with a practical example of his love, concern, and power. Their reaction is that of clearly converted followers.

I can approach this mystery imagining myself as one of the disciples, or as an observer. Or I can reflect on circumstances not at all related to the gospel story, but of the same genre that affect my life at this moment. I must remember that this same Jesus walks with me daily, as he does with all of us, and offers to enlighten my discouraged and confused mind and heart.

*

Reflecting on events from the gospels has great potential for our spiritual growth. When those events show a particular side of Jesus, such as the Wit and Wisdom Mysteries do, we may be inclined to take special pleasure in his having from time to time "won" a small battle in the larger war he waged with the Jewish leadership. Over the years they had manhandled the image of God and the place of religion downward into a relationship in which it was nearly impossible for love and compassion to be nurtured. It was law and hundreds of subdivisions of law that demanded a literal and stringent adherence to rubrical purity; the larger and more fundamental realities of the spiritual life were lost in the confusion.

In meditating on such events as those depicted in this set of mysteries, you can gain a greater appreciation for the mission of Jesus—to show the Father as God, not as a caricature of divinity created in humanity's image and likeness. The most consoling aspect of all this is that the Jesus who prevailed over his adversaries and challengers is the same Jesus who lives in us and in everyone today, ever ready to use the wit and wisdom he employed when useful to address issues we find ourselves unable to manage because we simply do not know how to approach them appropriately.

Search for other occasions in the gospels and apply your own preferences and experiences to perhaps an entirely new set for your use while praying the Rosary. It is certainly not out of place to include Our Lady in some or all of these events, vitally interested as she was in her son's mission and active as was her knowledgeable and supportive role in it.

Whatever the categories of wit and wisdom you choose to reflect upon while praying the Rosary, they will enrich your further reading of scripture and draw you always closer to the exemplary human that Jesus was in Israel and the God he is forever.

9

The Isaiah Mysteries

Isaiah is no stranger to us. Hailed as one of the most important and perceptive writers of the prophetic generations preceding Jesus' birth as one of us, Isaiah typifies the call, role, and impact of all the major and minor prophets whose writings are found in the canon of the Bible.

Those familiar with scripture recognize many passages from Isaiah. Chapters 1 to 39 are commonly identified as *Isaiah*, while chapters 40 to 66 are known as *Second Isaiah* or *Deutero-Isaiah* (also called the *Book of Consolation*). It seems to biblical scholars that two separate styles indicate that these sets of chapters are authored by different individuals, though the theme and import remain similar, suggesting the writers came out of the same or a similar prophetic community.

Prophets are too often narrowly defined as inspired to foresee important elements of salvation history and to summon the people of their time and place to a greater readiness to welcome God's kingdom of love and justice as it will be ushered in through the mediation of the promised Messiah. This definition is accurate enough, but beyond it—and in some instances far beyond it—the prophets are inspired by the Holy Spirit to call those they influence to a greater awareness of God's presence in their lives and to the repentance that recognition motivates along with the good works that flow naturally from conversion.

Isaiah's prophecy contains more recognizable expressions than any of the others—Daniel, Jeremiah, Amos, Jonah, Malachy, and the rest. It is from among these more commonly known portions of the prophecy that I have chosen verses to accompany the reflective praying of the Rosary, much as was done with the Psalms. Because there are more than enough quotations from the 66 chapters to construct several sets of *Isaiah Mysteries*, I have suggested three sets, the first taken from chapters 1–39, the second and third from chapters 40–66.

I also depart from the practice of identifying each mystery with its own title, as strictly speaking there are no titles that can be given to the quotations, each normally several lines in length. The principal means of identifying the passages is simply the chapter and verse where the quotation is found. My remarks following each quotation are quite brief, anticipating your desire to determine for yourself the essence of that on which you wish to reflect while praying.

Though Isaiah did not apply each passage found here specifically to the coming of the Messiah, in some manner each of the following verses does relate to Jesus and his life and purpose on earth. Your meditation could pursue that course. It could also follow the relationship each passage bears to your own life and circumstances. We all find ourselves somewhere and somehow in much of the book's contents.

Here are the three sets of Isaiah Mysteries:

The Isaiah Mysteries I (Isaiah)

Isaiah 1:16–17
Isaiah 1:18b–19

1. Isaiah 1:16–17

Wash yourselves; make yourselves clean;
remove the evil of your doings from before my eyes;
cease to do evil, learn to do good;
seek justice, rescue the oppressed, defend the orphan, plead for the widow.

Here begins the social justice message Isaiah so clearly champions. The words serve as a call to each of us to renew our dedication to seek out and do battle against systemic injustice in general and the specific forms of injustice we encounter where we live and work.

2. Isaiah 1:18b–19

Though your sins are like scarlet, they shall be like snow;
though they are red like crimson, they shall become like wool.
If you are willing and obedient, you shall eat the good of the land.

Openness to the inspirations of the Spirit, and readiness to respond in seeking and doing good create within our souls an atmosphere of conversion that recognizes how God accepts each of us unconditionally in love. As Paul later wrote, "If God is for us, who can be against us?" (Rm 8:31).

3. Isaiah 2:3

Many peoples shall come and say,
"Come, let us go up to the mountain of the Lord,
to the house of the God of Jacob;
that he may teach us his ways and that we may
walk in his paths."
For out of Zion shall go forth instruction,
and the word of the Lord from Jerusalem.

Sensitivity to God in our lives inspires us to seek God in everything so that we may learn God's way and God's will, and may follow the way and do the will. It is from the Holy City, which for Isaiah symbolizes God's real presence among us, that God's voice will speak and be heard.

4. Isaiah 2:4

He shall judge between the nations,
and shall arbitrate for many peoples;
they shall beat their swords into ploughshares,
and their spears into pruning hooks;
nation shall not lift up sword against nation,
neither shall they learn war any more.

The reign on earth of the kingdom of God's justice will see the inhabitants laying aside instruments of war and division. With God as mediator, only peace and harmony can result. We are invited to consider these words in their broader meaning and as applicable to our interior life, as well as to our local family and social situations. How do I settle disputes and differences with others? How, indeed, do I confront the warring elements within myself?

5. Isaiah 6:7–8

The seraph touched my mouth with [the coal] and said: "Now that this has touched your lips, your guilt has departed and your sin is blotted out."

Then I heard the voice of the Lord saying,"'Whom shall I send, and who will go for us?" And I said, "Here am I; send me!"

Isaiah's call from God and his symbolic preparation for his role as prophet pose questions for us about our own vocation as God's prophet in our time and place according to the circumstances crying out to be challenged. God prepares each of us to be an effective instrument in hastening along the coming of the kingdom, but we must be willing partners in that mission and say, as did Isaiah, "Here am I; send me."

The Isaiah Mysteries II (Second Isaiah)

Isaiah 40:3–5
Isaiah 40:10–11
Isaiah 40:28–31
Isaiah 42:6–7
Isaiah 43:1–2

2. Isaiah 40:3–5

A voice cries out:
"In the wilderness prepare the way of the Lord,
make straight in the desert a highway for our
*   God.*
Every valley shall be lifted up, and every
*   mountain and hill be made low;*
the uneven ground shall become level, and the
*   rough places a plain.*

> *Then the glory of the Lord shall be revealed,*
> *and all people shall see it together,*
> *for the mouth of the Lord has spoken.'*

In Handel's oratorio, *Messiah*, we encounter most of these words. In their prophetic scriptural context it seems Isaiah is saying justice and peace are the joint responsibility of God and humankind; together resolutions will be found and God acknowledged as author of all that is good. What do we see as our role in this continuous battle to straighten and level the road to true justice in our corner of the world?

2. Isaiah 40:10–11

> *See, the Lord God comes with might, and his arm*
> *rules for him;*
> *his reward is with him, and his recompense*
> *before him.*
> *He will feed his flock like a shepherd;*
> *he will gather the lambs in his arms, and carry*
> *them in his bosom,*
> *and gently lead the mother sheep.*

The image of the Good Shepherd we harbor comes as much from Isaiah as from Psalm 23. The poetic rhetoric should not obscure the heartening fact that, though God deals harshly with injustice in the world, those who seek and work for justice and peace will be sheltered and protected under God's providential care. Reflecting on this passage should be as consoling as it is challenging.

3. Isaiah 40:28–31

Have you not known? Have you not heard?
The Lord is the everlasting God, the Creator of
*   the ends of the earth.*
He does not faint or grow weary; his
*   understanding is unsearchable.*
He gives power to the faint, and strengthens the
*   powerless.*
Even youths will faint and be weary, and the
*   young will fall exhausted;*
but those who wait for the Lord shall renew their
*   strength,*
*   they shall mount up with wings like eagles,*
*   they shall run and not be weary,*
*   they shall walk and not faint.*

God's power is our power. If we work with and for God in the perpetual search for justice and peace in this world, however exhausting the process, we will have the strength to pursue it because the energy will come from God. This is another consoling passage, reminding us that though our efforts may at times seem futile, all things work for good when willed by the Creator.

4. Isaiah 42:6–7

> I am the Lord, I have called you in righteousness,
> I have taken you by the hand and kept you;
> I have given you as a covenant to the people, a
>   light to the nations,
>   to open the eyes that are blind,
>   to bring out prisoners from the dungeon,
>   from the prison those who sit in darkness.

Recognizable here are words similar to those Jesus quoted from Isaiah 61:1–2, in the synagogue in Nazareth, adding for his fellow Nazarenes that he was in fact the fulfillment of this prophecy. God calls us as well to be prophetic witnesses to the presence of God's kingdom on earth. God enables what God commands. We are guided as by a parent holding our hand as we cross dangerous thoroughfares. Our task is to serve others by bringing light, life, and freedom to them in whatever manner we are able to do so in those areas where we exert influence.

5. Isaiah 43:1–2

But now thus says the Lord,
he who created you, O Jacob,
he who formed you, O Israel:
Do not fear, for I have redeemed you;
I have called you by your name, you are mine.
When you pass through the waters, I will be with you;
and through the rivers, they shall not overwhelm you;
when you walk through fire you shall not be burned,
and the flame shall not consume you.

God assures us that we are individually known, loved, and protected by the One who created us in God's image and likeness, and that absolutely nothing can inhibit the relationship that exists between God and creature. To be called by name in Isaiah's time and culture was the sign someone was known intimately by another, and a degree of controlling ownership was assumed. God calls each of us by name, perhaps a name yet unknown to us. Belonging to God, we are assured of our future, whatever the circumstances that may challenge us in this life.

The Isaiah Mysteries III (Second Isaiah)

1. Isaiah 55:1–2

Ho, everyone who thirsts,
*   come to the waters;*
and you that have no money,
*   come, buy and eat!*
Come, buy wine and milk
*   without money and without price.*
Why do you spend your money for that which is
*   not bread,*
*   and your labor for that which does not satisfy?*
Listen carefully to me, and eat what is good,
*   and delight yourselves in rich food.*

This passage is read on more than one occasion during the liturgical year at the Eucharistic celebration. In it, God's continuous invitation to seek in God every good thing is revealed. The result will be our receiving freely and abundantly all that we need. Why waste time, energy, and resources worrying about our own welfare when God has us continuously in mind? We might inquire of ourselves whether our faith is in good working order.

2. Isaiah 55:6–7

Seek the Lord while he may be found,
*   call upon him while he is near;*
let the wicked forsake their way,
*   and the unrighteous their thoughts;*
let them return to the Lord, that he may have
*   mercy on them;*
*   and to our God, for he will abundantly pardon.*

Here we are issued a clear invitation to conversion. God is there to be found because God is never separated from us interiorly or exteriorly. Whatever in our lives needs to be changed or eradicated should be, and with God's grace can be, so that God may shower mercy on us as we return wholeheartedly to the abundant pardon and welcome only God is capable of giving us. Even our thoughts are fair game for repentance, as the next mystery tells us.

3. Isaiah 55:8–9

For my thoughts are not your thoughts,
*   nor are your ways my ways, says the Lord.*

For as the heavens are higher than the earth,
so are my ways higher than your ways
and my thoughts than your thoughts.

We need little explanation to understand the depth of meaning in these words Second Isaiah writes under God's inspiration. We are reminded of the immense chasm between humanity and divinity and how impotent we humans are trying to find our way unaided to God. This is a lesson in humility, due here because God has been bending over backward, so to speak, to illustrate how parent-like is God's love and care for creatures. As a result, we might be tempted to become overly familiar with our Creator if not actually take God for granted.

4. Isaiah 55:10–11

For as the rain and the snow come down from heaven,
  and do not return there until they have watered the earth,
making it bring forth and sprout,
  giving seed to the sower and bread to the eater,
so shall my word be that goes out from my mouth;

it shall not return to me empty,
   but it shall accomplish that which I purpose,
      and succeed in the thing for which I sent it.

One of the most beautiful passages in all of scripture, this consoling revelation assures us that God's word is alive, active, and powerful, and that when God speaks, whatever the message, that which God intends is accomplished. Jesus is God's Word, spoken in the Incarnation to all the earth. Jesus did not return to the Father until he had accomplished everything he was sent to do. Our life, our world itself, will not cease to seek fulfillment in accord with our creative purpose until that purpose has been accomplished; and it will be because God has said so.

5. Isaiah 61:1-2

The spirit of the Lord God is upon me,
   because the Lord has anointed me;
he has sent me to bring good news to the
      oppressed,
   to bind up the brokenhearted,
to proclaim liberty to the captives,
   and release to the prisoners;
to proclaim the year of the Lord's favor,

and the day of vengeance of our God;
to comfort all who mourn.

Even more thoroughly than Isaiah 42:6–7, these words identify Jesus' mission as he verbalized it in the reading from Isaiah in the Nazareth synagogue. Whoever suffers for whatever reason is the object of God's search so as to bring healing. But God works through us to effect the "year of the Lord's favor," just as the human Jesus exemplified. We must take Jesus as our model, scrutinizing his methods and making them ours. Praying the Rosary while meditating on these mysteries helps us keep in mind this clear objective.

*

You will have your own favorite passages from Isaiah—or any other prophetic voice of the Old Testament. Use these sets to become familiar with the mystery of God's association with creation, and appreciate how sensitive to God's Spirit Isaiah must have been to perceive within the inspiration he received such monumental expressions of loving care. Yes, God's justice demands that it be replicated on earth through our efforts; yet, God's mercy conquers all, and we who attempt to live in habitual orientation toward God are heartened by the continual repetition of God's intent to be with us and hold us safe from the dangers to which we might succumb in this world.

As a portion of scripture already available to the people of Jesus' time, there is no doubt opportunities arose in the home at Nazareth for Jesus and his parents to discuss the meaning and implications of such passages as Isaiah writes. How did Mary interpret the words of the prophet as more and more clearly she realized her son was someone special to God? Did Jesus and Mary—after Joseph's death and as Jesus' leaving home neared—converse over these and other prophetic writings, wondering if and how they could apply to him and his mission? Meditating on the Isaiah Mysteries affords us the opportunity to consider every angle of involvement and understanding our minds can manufacture. We ought not to let the occasion pass without taking advantage of it.

10

Other Alternative Mysteries

The preceding chapters have introduced and expanded on the concept of alternative mysteries. They are meant to accompany your recitation of the Rosary, helping to enable you to broaden the field of possibilities for reflection or meditation well beyond the traditional Glorious, Sorrowful, and Joyful mysteries along with the Pope's new Luminous Mysteries.

In some detail I have suggested more than a dozen collections of events, circumstances, considerations, or themes that lend themselves in sets of five to serve as *mysteries* from which you can draw useful and beneficial experiences in devotional prayer.

Proposed as mysteries were those entitled Wondrous, Vocation, Golden Rule, Rites of

Passage, Hidden Life, Wit and Wisdom, four sets from the Psalter, and three from Isaiah.

There are, of course, more. Without belaboring the ones already mentioned, or intending to suggest the traditional Glorious, Sorrowful, and Joyful mysteries are overused and outdated—on the contrary!—I will conclude by proposing other topics or titles that can be followed up at the convenience of the reader. The first set will be elaborated upon minimally by way of example.

A Personal Favorite: The Ghana Mysteries

I spent a significant part of my active life as a teacher and administrator in Ghana, West Africa. Before it gained its independence in 1957, Ghana was a British colony known as the Gold Coast.

During my years there, I observed that Ghanaians, like most sub-Saharan peoples, hold an ontological and anthropological approach to life that differs notably from that of dwellers in the northern hemisphere, particularly Europe and North America. That fact, far from being negative, has much to recommend it. I isolated five particular aspects of Ghanaian life in which this difference is significant, and rationalized their usefulness as reflections for praying the Rosary. What is more, I found they could apply also to Jesus' life.

The five areas are: appreciation of and great respect for (1) ancestors, (2) nature, (3) time, (4) constructive dialogue in problem-solving situations, and (5) hospitality. Jesus can be seen to have had a lively sensitivity to these same realities, and he knew how to live in a balanced relationship with them, as most Ghanaians do. We "northerners" tend to develop a less respectful relationship in these areas because we are inclined to be more oriented toward objects that are user-friendly than toward persons—where mutuality is a given—and this emerges in our system of values.

Using these topics, I can reflect on how Jesus reveres, respects, and is attentive to the influence of his human ancestors and elders. He enjoys, appreciates, respects, and protects nature. He values and uses time properly and productively. He understands the purpose of constructive confrontation and knows when and how to use it to advantage. And he offers hospitality freely, and just as freely accepts it.

I don't propose this set of mysteries for those unfamiliar with sub-Saharan cultures, though the concepts related to these themes might appeal to some if applied in an appropriately personal context. My objective here is to suggest there are similar themes arising from your personal experience, and from it you may wish to pursue the structuring of complementary mysteries that have greater meaning for you.

Others in Thumbnail Sketch

Seeking the mysterious but very real influence of God in human life by means of the comfortable and familiar form of the Rosary as prayer—though using different meditations— can be surprisingly enriching.

The suggestions given below may serve to invite you to formulate similar sets that contain personally meaningful and potentially enriching reflections for growth in your spiritual life. The objective in taking such liberties with a long-standing and virtually unchanged popular devotion is so that new life and enthusiasm can be breathed into a proven and much loved prayer. As the U.S. bishops reminded us in 1973, "we can freely experiment. New sets of mysteries are possible." (Cf. quotation, p. 3) These and like topics can be imagined and subjected to experimentation in your praying of the Rosary. There is no limit to potentially appropriate materials as mysteries.

Thinking of developing the following in sets of five, consider these possibilities:

- Deceased persons who were influential in your life
- Influential persons still living
- Other relatives, friends, colleagues, teachers, etc., living or deceased
- Occasions of special joy in my life
- Challenging, difficult, or painful occasions in my life
- Gospel personalities sympathetic to Jesus
- Gospel personalities inimical to Jesus
- Events from today's news; how would Jesus respond to each event?
- Parables of Jesus most meaningful to me
- Personalities from the New Testament canticles (Simeon, Mary, Elizabeth, John the Baptist, Zachary)
- Personalities from the parables who were "winners"
- Personalities from the parables who were "losers"

- Books that have changed my life
- Places that have impacted my life
- Unanswered questions/mysteries of my family/community/work place that have influenced my life
- Locations (scenes) of particularly impressive beauty I have lived at or visited
- Moments of sudden awakening to awareness
- Gifts of personality or skill I possess
- Musical compositions most meaningful to me
- Works of art that have moved me
- Natural or human-made designs that impress me
- Surprises that have awakened me to God's providential goodness

These suggested alternative sets of mysteries clearly go far beyond the original and longstanding mysteries proposed by the church for the consideration of the faithful when praying the Rosary.

No disrespect is intended in seeking, proposing, or using such alternatives. Rather, they are seen to be complementary to the Glorious, Sorrowful, and Joyful mysteries in that they spring from them, elaborate on them, and draw attention to parallel, peripheral, or related persons, places, events, and characteristics found in the traditional mysteries and update them. Nothing relative to the eternal Jesus and the "economy of salvation" can be foreign or out of place to the individual who seriously seeks to enhance his or her comprehension of the awesome reality of God-with-us in our world and how the ongoing presence of the Spirit offers an infallible opportunity to grow by virtue of the immense impact that awareness of that Presence can provide. This assertion has been forcefully affirmed by Pope John Paul II throughout his encyclical on the Rosary. The role of Mary in all of this is, in itself, more than sufficient to justify reflection and prayer using her Rosary.

Aids to prayer are devised to *en*able, not *dis*able. When the Rosary no longer attracts, challenges, or offers a positive response from a prayerful person who has felt comfortable with popular devotions in the past, it is time to examine the devotion and ask whether by creative and purposeful means the form of prayer can be brought back into active use to the spiritual advantage of the one praying. I believe the answer to that is a resounding *yes*!

Philip Armstrong, C.S.C., is a teacher, missionary, author, and religious brother in the Congregation of Holy Cross. His ministry to the church has brought him to serve in Texas, Michigan, Ghana, New Mexico, and Notre Dame, Indiana. He has served as Provincial Superior to the Midwest Province in Indiana, and as Assistant to the Superior General of the Congregation in Rome. Br. Armstrong was born and raised in South Bend, Indiana, where he resides today.